AMERICAN ANTHEM

A SONG OF OUR NATION

Words by *Gene Scheer*

Art by

Fahmida Azim, Elizabeth Baddeley, Matt Faulkner, Michelle Lee, Rafael López, Veronica Miller Jamison, Christine Almeda, Edel Rodriguez, James McMullan, Laura McGee Kvasnosky & Kate Harvey McGee, London Ladd, and Jacqueline Alcántara

PHILOMEL

PHILOMEL BOOKS
An imprint of Penguin Random House LLC, New York

First published in the United States of America by Philomel Books,
an imprint of Penguin Random House LLC, 2021

Visit us online at penguinrandomhouse.com.

Library of Congress Cataloging-in-Publication Data is available.

Printed in the USA
ISBN 9780593465547
10 9 8 7 6 5 4 3 2 1

Edited by Jill Santopolo and Talia Benamy
Design by Ellice M. Lee
Text set in Hoefler Text

To Kristina, with my love.
—*Gene Scheer*

To my ammu and abbu,
you came to America dreaming your kid would have a medical license, a bajillion dollars,
and a paid-off mortgage, but got this book dedication instead.
—*Fahmida Azim*

Dedicated to the memory of my Aunt Ann—
a woman who had a deep love for her country and wove her stories from her heart.
—*Elizabeth Baddeley*

For my Kris. Always.
—*Matt Faulkner*

In memory of my halmoni, Hyang-Nan Wee—
a woman who relished spicy cold noodles and sweets, who embodied strength, courage,
and perseverance, and who became an American citizen at the age of seventy-six.
—*Michelle Lee*

To dream chasers.
—*Rafael López*

For my grandmothers—Veronica and Ruby Lee—and the women
who birthed and raised them—Cecilia, Priscilla Inez, and Lucy.
—*Veronica Miller Jamison*

For my mom, Reza, generous in faith and hope.
—*Christine Almeda*

For my parents, Cesareo and Coralia Rodriguez—
their risks in search of freedom gave me life.
—*Edel Rodriguez*

For Arthur and Lily.
—*James McMullan*

To the growers and grocers, gardeners and gleaners.
—*Laura McGee Kvasnosky & Kate Harvey McGee*

To my one and only mother, Victoria—I love and miss you every day.
—*London Ladd*

For all who call this country home.
—*Jacqueline Alcántara*

All we've been given
By those who came before
The dream of a nation
Where freedom would endure

The work and prayers
Of centuries
Have brought us to this day
What shall be our legacy?
What will our children say?

Let them say of me
I was one who believed
In sharing the blessings
I received

Let me know in my heart
When my days are through
America
America
I gave my best to you

Each generation

From the plains to distant shore

With the gifts that they were given

Were determined to leave more

Valiant battles fought together
Acts of conscience fought alone

These are the seeds
From which America has grown

Let them say of me
I was one who believed
In sharing the blessings
I received

Let me know in my heart
When my days are through
America
America
I gave my best to you

For those who think
They have nothing to share
Who fear in their hearts
There is no hero there

Know each quiet act of dignity

Is that which fortifies

The soul of a nation
That never dies

Let them say of me
I was one who believed
In sharing the blessings
I received

Let me know in my heart
When my days are through

America
America
I gave my best to you

1. All we've been given
   By those who came before
   The dream of a nation
   Where freedom would endure

   The work and prayers
   Of centuries
   Have brought us to this day
   What shall be our legacy?
   What will our children say?

   Let them say of me
   I was one who believed
   In sharing the blessings
   I received

   Let me know in my heart
   When my days are through
   America
   America
   I gave my best to you

2. Each generation
   From the plains to distant shore
   With the gifts that they were given
   Were determined to leave more

   Valiant battles fought together
   Acts of conscience fought alone
   These are the seeds
   From which America has grown

   Let them say of me
   I was one who believed
   In sharing the blessings
   I received

   Let me know in my heart
   When my days are through
   America
   America
   I gave my best to you

3. For those who think
   They have nothing to share
   Who fear in their hearts
   There is no hero there

   Know each quiet act of dignity
   Is that which fortifies
   The soul of a nation
   That never dies

   Let them say of me
   I was one who believed
   In sharing the blessings
   I received

   Let me know in my heart
   When my days are through
   America
   America
   I gave my best to you

American Anthem

Words and Music by
GENE SCHEER

Moderato

All we've been gi - ven by those who came be-fore, the— dream of a na - tion where

free - dom would en - dure. The— work and prayers of cen - tu - ries have brought us to this day.

What shall be our leg - a - cy? What will our child - ren say? Let them

say of me I was one___ who be - lieved in— shar - ing the bless - ings

I re - ceived. Let me know in my heart when my days___ are___ through, A -

me - ri - ca, A - me - ri - ca, I gave my best to you.

FAHMIDA AZIM has illustrated many books, including her award-winning debut, *Muslim Women Are Everything*. Fahmida lives and creates in Seattle, Washington. Find her work at fahmida-azim.com and follow her on Twitter and Instagram @fahmida_azim.

ELIZABETH BADDELEY is the illustrator of many books about extraordinary people, including the *New York Times* bestselling *I Dissent*. She's happiest out exploring the world with her sketchbook, but has spent much of the COVID-19 pandemic learning how to sew. Elizabeth lives in Kansas City, Missouri, with her husband, young son, and assortment of furry friends. You can visit her online at ebaddeley.com and follow her on Instagram @eabaddeley.

MATT FAULKNER has crafted the words and pictures for over forty books for children. He loves to create work for books that are both historic and fantastic in nature and strives to not get them confused. Matt lives with his wife, author Kristen Remenar, and their kids and cat in the lower right-hand corner of the Michigan mitten. Matt invites you to come hang out at his website: mattfaulkner.com.

MICHELLE LEE is a Korean-American illustrator from Los Angeles whose work includes *My Love for You Is Always* by Gillian Sze and *Chloe's Lunar New Year* by Lily LaMotte. Michelle finds inspiration in nature, her family, and memories from childhood. Keep up with her online at mklillustration.com!

RAFAEL LÓPEZ is an internationally recognized artist who has illustrated numerous acclaimed picture books, including *Just Ask! Be Different, Be Brave, Be You* by Sonia Sotomayor; *Dancing Hands: How Teresa Carreño Played the Piano for President Lincoln* by Margarita Engle; and *The Day You Begin* by Jacqueline Woodson, among others. He resides in San Diego and Central Mexico. You can visit him at rafaellopez.com.

VERONICA MILLER JAMISON is an illustrator and surface pattern designer living in Philadelphia. Trained as a fashion designer, Veronica has created art and patterns for Hallmark, *Essence* magazine, and Lilly Pulitzer. She is the illustrator of *A Computer Called Katherine*, written by Suzanne Slade, and *This Is a School*, written by John Schumacher, aka "Mr. Schu." To see more of her work, find her online at veronicajamisonart.com and on Instagram @veronicajamisonart.

CHRISTINE ALMEDA is a Filipino-American freelance illustrator and character designer from New Jersey. She has a love for children's books and has worked on various chapter books. Christine believes in the power of creativity and diverse storytelling and knows that art can make life more beautiful. You can visit her online at www.christinealmeda.com and find her on Twitter and Instagram @eychristine.

EDEL RODRIGUEZ was born in Havana, Cuba, and raised in El Gabriel, a small town surrounded by fields of tobacco and sugarcane. In 1980, Rodriguez and his family left for America during the Mariel boatlift. They settled in Miami, where Rodriguez was introduced to American pop culture for the first time. Social justice, poster art, and Western advertising are all aspects of his life that continue to inform his work. You can visit Edel online at edelrodriguez.com and find him on Twitter @edelstudio and on Instagram @edelrodriguez.

JAMES McMULLAN has created images for magazines, books for adults and children, animated films, and US stamps, but he is most well known for his over eighty posters for Lincoln Center Theater as well as his illustrated memoir, *Leaving China*. You can find James online at jamesmcmullan.com and follow him on Instagram @jamesmcmullanart.

Sisters **LAURA McGEE KVASNOSKY** and **KATE HARVEY McGEE** grew up in Sonora, California. They first came to love the beauty of America there in the Sierra foothills and learned the importance of First Amendment rights and the Fourth Estate from their father, who flew a huge American flag over his Main Street newspaper office. Kate is a noted pastel painter and lives in Oregon's Coast Range. Laura lives in Seattle and is the award-winning creator of more than twenty books for children. They illustrated the last three together: *Little Wolf's First Howling*, *Squeak!*, and *Ocean Lullaby*. You can visit them online at khmland.com (for Kate) and LMKBooks.com (for Laura).

LONDON LADD has illustrated numerous critically acclaimed children's books. He uses a unique mixed media approach, combining cut paper textured with acrylic paint, tissue paper, colored pencil, pen, and ink, and touches of digital to bring his diverse subjects to life. Each image is steeped in intensity and emotion, a reflection of the artist himself. You can find London at londonladd.com and follow him on Instagram @london.ladd.

JACQUELINE ALCÁNTARA is the award-winning and critically acclaimed illustrator of *The Field* by Baptiste Paul, *Freedom Soup* by Tami Charles, *Jump at the Sun* by Alicia D. Williams, and *Your Mama* by NoNieqa Ramos. Her books have been listed as best books of the year by multiple trade outlets, named to the Kids' IndieNext list, and received multiple starred reviews. You can find Jacqueline's website at jacquelinealcantara.com, or follow her on Twitter and Instagram @_jacqueline_ill.